Rebecca letters

To Sharon

August 97

Seattle

Cajun

Rebecca letters

Laynie Browne

KELSEY ST. PRESS

Also by Laynie Browne:
Hereditary Zones (Boog Literature 1993)
One Constellation (Leave Books 1994)

The author wishes to thank the editors of the following journals where selections from this book first appeared: *AVEC, Chain, No Roses Review, Phoebe,* and *The Washington Review.*

Library of Congress Cataloging-in-Publication Data
Browne, Laynie, 1966–
      Rebecca letters / Laynie Browne.
            p.   cm.
      ISBN 0-932716-43-1
      I. Title.
PS3552.R748R43   1997   97–9462
811'.54–dc21   CIP

Book design by Poulson/Gluck Design
Text set in Adobe Caslon
Printed by West Coast Print Center

Kelsey St. Press P.O. Box 9235, Berkeley, California 94709
phone 510-845-2260   fax 510-548-9185   email: kelseyst@sirius.com
web site: http://www.sirius.com/~kelseyst/welcome.html

Distributed by: Small Press Distribution   800-869-7553
                   Bookpeople   800-999-4650

NATIONAL ENDOWMENT FOR THE ARTS   Publication of this book was made possible in part by grants from the National Endowment for the Arts and the California Arts Council.

For my grandmother,
Eva Leiter 1911–1993

Contents

Rebecca Letters

"Whenever an order for a coffin came,
Hazel went to tell the bees who was dead"

— Mary Webb

Mailed heart Monday. Luminary pond. In day and age who is:

Sub reverie, who to tell the dead.

The story of the ghost. The story of Rebecca. The question of color in lightness and dark. The black mirror and other inconsistencies.

There is the sound of verbosity. These heavy new pages. The sound of skin, and the dream which is sent in small increments.

And when one is sitting too close to you, what does one do? That time of year when bramble dogs and pigeons ulterior. Leaves, pockets. Warm enough to stop on the street.

Curations where there is no spelling, or inscriptions to create a secret language.

Still rather having or habit split apart once while walking.

Walking is perhaps the most dangerous occupation. Either that or waking.

Mood twisted sway. This underworld where I speak of you. A tree is surrender to both earth and sky. A tree is anything but dormant. I am not wishing the sky away.

Letters, utterance, perplexities— Thoughts manifest everything made of thoughts. Reflexive atmosphere. Which means thought comes from matter and the opposite.

He asks about my hands. In everything touch present.

I am not answering the waterfall sent so that I would be barely able to stand.

There are calls I am not answering and others wishing to be received. There is asking your origins.

I fear I am in love with a phantom. You've already answered this question.

But how did we arrive at the place where you were bandaging?

He asks about my hands. In everything touch present.

To tell the story one must begin somewhere. First you were first. You appeared to me in a dream. This is not the actual order, but the first event of which I knew. In the dream I am standing by the stove, boiling water to make an infusion. A clearing as if a pond. The color of an evenly overcast day. Not oppressive or mute, but just enough cloud so as not to be startled by the bright clarity. Luminous grey. You asked me what I was doing. Why else would your gaze be woven into my acts? You told me to drink water. You convinced me of the necessity of such.

Lost scatters. A door bell door. Sidelong memory: you alongside.

This is the memory of days in Providence with weather watching one's internal state. The body retracts and reinvents. Sidewalk mimics sky.

I dream of this other history. The history of luminosity. A history of what is like a moon. The luminary pond. Inability to recall one's element is the same as being lost in an apothecary. Lost between aromas. A _____ is setting. Her description is brimming. She is phosphorous. The name of the book is kept secret. Not an idol.

The village is no longer diaphanous. The heads of tenements lilt.

A drift stairwell mapped answering the voice. Abundance sleeps the missing violin.

A relationship between gazing and memorization of hedges.

Storm pebble.

Pictures same lace in the tempestuous shoestring.

There is a sinking line of stars around the neckline. There is a drowning word of seas which carries candles and burning things.

Emblems sewn into the breastplate, worn and carefully tended.

If there were one yielding source would the clouds looking down project beings as such, or would electricity span skies in spectral waves enlightening what was drawn towards the window?

When once a heart mender had traveled abruptly stirred, livid remembrance. Her appearance the spidery enactment. Rewoven carried a thread. Filigree re-encapsulated dream time.

The lash. The last accomplished which returns hands in lap or in this early register map as countless prism ash. The circlingness so knowledge. Which is or hauntingly ash. As if there could be anything less than as the tide, or less immediately breakers and then to sleep. If a recording could be sent let me enfold this or this. A sliding ontology. This is also now.

What they have in common is also without parameters.

A shell broken by fire.

The alarming habit of traveling far to meet those who grew up in my home. What does this signify? The relation between betweens. Distance, proximity illusions.

To sleep on ashes.

How to sight a storm. There was one lost in woods or trees in other worlds. You wandered. And the name of the street where you lived.

The kind of latch statements which can rescue. Anything beyond thought and hand.

The deciding factor would be to seal and stamp it or not. Was I walking and somehow not present? Belonging to themselves, the trees not having these conversations.

I was trying to be tranquil. And then windmills or storm vehicles clouded my view. I was trying to sleep in that submerged hallway where once the quiet waters were quiet and less mirrors. Where once quietly, as if it were possible to sleep in a pool. I was once less than wading but within the lack of return, something woke. The embrace of a balmy atmosphere. And climate has everything to do. So that everything clutched without pretense. There was little or no pressure. And still the barometer dropped. We held between us enough to drink fluently. And less calmly was I able to sleep, after swimming in the actual sea. This sea was calm but also clear. All was visible. There was a map at the bottom of the waters in coral and shrines. In fish undulations and salt. I had spent a large part of the summer in some cave while not reading the book which I thought was in front of me. I thought I had constructed and arranged the words. I thought within talk of illumination. Spectral lightning. The kind of truth easily swallowed behind the pleasing array of seafan. Behind the whirl of intentions skirting edges. Behind the lazy heat which permeates icecubes. Sunken in sand where once brightness could no longer conceal this underwater map. Where other modes of locomotion drift. Even lying motionless along the surface of the waters was brimming. Even drifting to sleep there was the presence of wakefulness.

As if to learn sleep through observation. No difficulty sleeping, misses much of meaningful sleep. For this reason the plan to dream all of those things awake still resistant to tide flows. Or floodlights.

There is a web to be reunited. Fastening through one each center as proceeding, hands one on top of the other to contain fragments or suspend a tide of inner tendencies. Caverns beneath wakeful dreams, emptying of intimate matter, and the fallen forms of trees which lie beside, twirl around their roots.

Behind the opening hill is forehead's diameter etched in satin purse. Where winter discerns the rules of winter, where the meaning of the protagonist is a different subject from where the subject arrives.

It was the place where time became the wrist and not anything strung or worn as an armlet. Here was the dream running in snow from something which seemed important.

Both had illusions which later became snow. Hers was that the snow would not be cold. She saw it as powder. He fixed the image of cotton and added another miscalculation, assuming powdered sugar would also be sweet. There was no taste in the image. Only the cold wet was disappointed, as the sharpness of ice.

To awaken from both of these proclivities, time might surround them like a snowstorm. Arriving in the distant hills of a forehead memory.

Is there a dependable urn into which I might deposit the results of all that has been burned?

Could it be that our feet fell at any given time into the same exact patterns in earth so that I was walking within a hologram of your image?

After another story unhinged, her radiance gone out amidst darkness. I saw this across a table calmly stir in tea. Too far from a sourcepoint, like my shadow in trees. The walking, wading, scrying image visits. As all those painted letters flutter to the floor.

(*Impressions upon the earth recorded in walking.*)

For those fearing gravity where is a place to dwell among harmonic strangers? For those with no trees in their eyes, where to find a mirror of seasons? Where to sleep willingly in the presence of sensationless being?

There seems to be a natural law, that the more one moves with purpose beyond what can be seen or possessed, the more the house steps out supporting. The more less matterful minds are orchestrating a den of heavy consent and concentration, the more wings despite crushing. The more one eye in eye is distant yet clear, the more sensation can be trusted and the safer the body will dwell amidst circumstances subject to the limitations of preoccupation, undulation, foreknowledge.

Knowing in sensation cannot be acquired, but can be concentrated from the tips of fingers, so that what moves out from fingertips which contain seasonless design, is the manifestation of thought. We are mostly made of thought, not water. The watery interplay between resolution, and the float which sustains positive drift.

As the streets expand and contract, pulsations of weather twist the meaning of season.

With reversed perspective in embracing, traveling towards a different future or past.

The diagonal shadow of October light falling across, seems to cross all in this manner. Parts remaining in shadow are the instances where inner vision remains submerged and not brought out with the shards of mirror above ground.

She touched my back again. *The place is sleeping.* And the flood for the place which had slept washed through city rooms, until floors were dark with mud and transforming coolness of waves. The kind one can only accept silently, as dormant space retreats into night. As windows purple to maps, as the spine again is transfigured, a dark bird in rain.

I was walking towards some tower lit from within a lavender cloud. I was walking, as always walking through steps in black which lead towards what must be a remarkable departure from all that has come before. Toward this corner of mysterious sky where someone once imagined a peak which would appear from a distance, a suspended locket.

Sage messengers certain accomplices know this.

Sage spell works, and who calls what is matter (or to speak blindly) in what is suspended time.

The smoke which unfurls, and then wait.

In the photograph she is holding a doll upright, standing, as if presenting a companion.

There are wings spilling from paper, lanterns between hands, dreams in which the tears became reflections of eyesight. Seeing which ignites the wings which had carried his body. Dreams in which in order to awaken, something else was denied. Dreams in which the vehicle of air was transformed into chariot. Speech in which the silence included gaps which later became fountains. And maps which follow this spilling.

Where wings became fern or soil. Reflections in which fountains continued to fill the space occupied by a tree, and something else was denied. In order to walk, in order to return color to faces where water and air, a cleansing.

Where substance meets the diagrams of dreams in which the space occupied by a body could not be met, the drafts disintegrate. Plans curl up in blue edges. No lines can be drawn to represent substance. No silence is the empty space of landscape between meetings.

Dream fills these edges with happenings. Happenings will fill these meetings with air. And something else was determined, that the water rushing upwards made the same sounds as his rushing. That the air colliding had the same force as a meeting. That there can be no gaps in weather that remains proximate. That we are breathing in collaboration with all intimate matter.

In the park I deliberately pass this shadow. She stands on top of the cement canopy of the water fountain, branches around her white arms. On each of her four edges is one word.

Which twists a limit in this coming snow. Movement brings bliss. Include the walking priestess in letters.

Thoughts of tripping reveries, stones or singing water. Pulsations in my hand.

She who dwells in sourcepoint.

The tea is sweet and becoming a cauldron. This whirlpool centers wishing. This wishing container which has been calmly dredged. And the remains of plants which have given their substance to water.

Where substance meets thirst is absence. Where absence calls reverie smears. Where smudges call accuracy illusion. Where illusion unusually uncovers a meeting. Where meetings are vertical estuaries. Where rivers continue in substance. Where substance in form is imagined. Where imaginings lead back to absence. Where remembering is presence each moon turns in. Where turning is no obligatory surface. Where surfaces remain no place to live. Where residence dwells in meetings.

All that she has is something she has gathered.

A game in which the value of a hand is of greater value than a hand held by others.

There is no way to unhinge a story.

Obscurity is the history of obscure history.

Repeating the mind of silence in latitude:

These scurrying days
blinking nights.

I admire the quality of light in January when to look down from the skies is to be within a cathedral. The late afternoon becomes a medieval forest. Buildings are the heaviness of plague and ominous rushing vehicles. Feet move beyond black city surfaces. I wear a conglomeration of amulets for protection. There is the sense of a priestess traveling by lamplight. The light held between hands in warming themselves. And stepping into so many overheated interiors. Layers of velvet trailing behind. The ritual of boiling waters and scented resins. The ritual covering of head and heels. The head is carried carefully if not to be frozen.

If all things in a book are impossible, how were they possibly written? His face reminds me of his face. In any case I lament, or try to stop lamenting. This is impossible and yet it has been written. Written countlessly, spoken silently, to the air.

The fear is an approximate guise. It is actually a fear of intangibles. There are natural laws which prevent such occurrences. It is not possible to give himself any other way.

The fear of possibilities can never be trusted. He saw only the desire which became a fence and a fencepost. He is unaware of the dangers of walking.

I have been at this station before. Rushing by my hands cannot even motion or complain in their inability to form shapes. This is the place of oncoming, which as sideswiped in waiting coats and gleaming tracks. This is under the ground a place which has been dug out by other hands which appear fleetingly in the silver motion of derailment. The other ways seem less difficult, and yet they are unknown.

The darkness of the day is moist swamp news.

Or curling circlets of rain.

Radial birds in combination with leaves are not replenished.

A humming dropped these bending mists and the sound is sweeping along tarantula.

Confidences in sporadic mugs. I am nearly walking now. Rain is a curtain and eyes are parted from what could be partnering. You are nearly walking beside me. I dreamed of spiral rooted trees, labyrinth trunks in sinuous brown cords and waves. And this looked nothing and everything like a maze. The only transit which can occur in memory. I was looking out the window, an unfamiliar frame. To follow the arc of those many spines which grew upwards and downwards. The backs transplanting. It is easiest to be lost in these acres of sound. It is most pleasant to wake on their edges.

I noticed the park shadow scrying, and gave her your name, for the sake of her gaze.

There is this walking priestess, walking through what was a statue, an ancestor, a phoneme unnamed.

As the waters also scrying her eyes. In search of distant history, utter reflection. A gaze mirrors maze.

Gone, gone, gone beyond gone.

City interests precipitous, as one stands in a doorway, a storefront looking. So excuses multiply to walk a certain way.

Describe the city box. There is a cost for the culmination of walls. You can buy this semi space with your smallness. You can crawl between walking as a window recalls what else is unlatched. A fire escape doubles green or pigeons born too young to fly, too large to be carried.

Epiphany scatters

Place hand on chest to hold shards.

The statue in the branches is holding a pitcher in one hand, a small bowl to her face with the other, searching the skies as seen in water.

Seven refractions of shattered reflection.

How many breaths approach the dream, then circle back apparatus in time.

Stratosphere collaboration.

New moon intention spurned new cloudy remembrance.

Don't blow out that which was lit as intention. There was an ocean on her fingers and still would not extinguish.

You must actually touch the wick, sweeping away some visible fog.

The ridged wing of a shell

Feathered tip of flame

Calendula brightens the gold season

Ship sense calenders mimic tide

She walks across these drawn boxes, dwellings and days, the salt of retrievances. To walk across a calendar is the same as the shadow in the trees. She appears fixed and yet her dress is not calm, she appears to be the same color as herself. Such stone white arms.

Hurled a pillow aside in which not being finished with delirium. Smudging continuously. A book in which to dwell. The smoke curls up from the shell.

Looking forward, a disentangling, or dismemberment of form.

Conversing with elements.

The shell is also a palm, also a frond. Her neck is also a universe.

There are meters in the season beyond what is driven ephemeral. I cannot describe the sense of walking through these trees. On the floor holding a jar linden blossoms were dizzying as nerves sleep easily. And now it is almost a return to this spoke on the wheel, the death of the year in October masks. In the card which is the shaman who is experience, who maintains one face beneath a face in order to endure the fleeting century of grief.

Grief tea, brew in waves, the throat a vessel. This lavender, this rose, the red clover blossom gathered my hand in May. They expand to float garlands. Color absorbing intention. This time of departing. This mirror float of what can be known only through a window. Of what can be internalized in the form of plant intelligence.

Ally hawthorne, guardian of the hinge. Opens what remains closed. Closes that which has been open. The many gates are armatures, the many flags which appear and reappear, the body of seepage of directional tide. And when reversed the heart gate, eyes glowingly close, fingers reach proddingly to know the new body, to sense the new rhythm of ambulation. When reversed arms are not lying at sides. Fingers are conduits into air depending on the formation, direction.

Spiny teachings of protection.

One drop on sourcepoint. A way to taste the changer.

What is alterative, that which changes everything and no knowing why. Worn in a pouch around the heart. This is the heavy medicine of bearing. The continuous circling of thought which can be removed with a glance at a flower, which can be placed again on the altar as the thirst which quenches miles.

The larger deciphering begins with setting names. They disappear over streetlight, the promising matches, leaves below knees. A rush of shadows blend to disentangle from what were dreams of scattered ash. The space takes all of facing itself; it is the desire to take in what is not talk, or misdirection, or ghost. The season bedroom said I can no longer. There is no bedroom, and I can no longer torch the bed. The more space claiming so receding is retreating. No longer gazing at the indecipherable legend.

Cards confirm the lovers, just out of the oven;
root which dissolves. They are not seeking
ances but wish to have acknowledged that v
sustaining, that which is all that remains to be
the rushing of distress.

The house is constructed of watery images. Th
creatures half in shell. A spill which can be
into or out of shelling, which can be seen as
contained.

Ancestor Alphabets

Those who have left have taken their tracks and placed them behind themselves in a different direction. This orientation describes the sky. Bridges are collapsed and dragged between distances I'd never seen. Suddenly water was visible beneath, and all of the trouble of breathing was relocated to another organ. A mind with an eye carries the voice of a spine. Nothing is unmistakable. Distances see themselves, gasp. Electricity changed again, the seventh course of the day between hands and eyes. This redness began as some envy of sunset. Every word was a child.

The darkest mood was hidden in a matchbox. The tiny oars move as if within fire, and the cat closes her eye and watches the mild box sway in transparent rain. Window ledges remember who has been here. Beg walls, and the back becomes an arch. Hands were meant as bare thermometers.

Cauldron ring of saffron myrrh began colonies in glass jars. Something within had watered a star. The sound of reflections is mimicking. What had gathered beside her: one in waves who remembers a lamppost. This is the way the paintings wept: one way of moving a ship. Letters await to answer those scars, or those who had left a burning oar. There is a waterless script which is forgiving.

The place is a whipswitch. Thirst is cloving pantomime. Plants in the male June had named certain weather. Her electricity was changed in circuits of rain. Within a landscape, it was the contact of known skin. From a ditch the letters were thrown up onto the land above, until a new alphabet was created which could be seen by birds. It is not only what was thrown up, but their impressions in the ground, and that they could have crawled away, and then we would have been left again with a scarless landscape, and all that was remaining to be said.

We will soon be building a see-through school.

The intention was to watch the owl within the side-wise waterfan.

There is a habit of marking rivers by walking years beyond a source.

A new river begins with a belly instead of a bank.

A table became an altarway. River rapids became the only place to move rapidly. Clouds could be carried to an endpoint. Recalling a place that later became a fist, her namesake dissolved in water. A gem became a song that kept repeating its facets into diagrams, where light hit a low note.

If you place your body in that series of postures, you send a message.

Something else scatters radiance.

No venus-lookinglass could disappoint the sand in a hour.

The sound of waves had scurried to ask their temper-
ature. This is the same as asking myself the shape
of the words as my hands mail the letters. No one
had ever seen thirst, but the unmistakable landscape
gathered visions of waterwells. Upon first reading, a
story of exchanged letters appeared romantic. Later
a source spoke that it couldn't have been so. The
letters were written to avoid conversation.

I watched a circle walk

A walled memorabilia sank forth each sundry sun

Air and breath were born in one stroke

and so the brush struggled on through tresses

of trees, and into the tangle of belonging.

A calendar of lavender inflects the second of June.

Soporific is the difference between true sleep and mimicking time. For fear of not finding a doorway, the adequate lull is to remember a place above a doorway. Corner each blue of candlemass sky. Two moons beginning silence of black fly capillaries. The original bed, was a bed of sand. Precisely as the sky can be seen on an island, so that the approach of a storm which had been created through letters became an imagined landscape hovering weightless between the eyes.

A place of rest, not only of the mind, but the eye, is a lake which lies down swiftly in her undergarments, drowning in the calm gloss of dawn, the green pitch of morning, and the gleam once thought to be chlorophyll, or a dress drawn in hedges and backstroke. A river amulet which water had covered.

Speak A Long While
To A Brook

"*From the evidence, it appears that Alice Rowlands pretended to be able to levitate herself and the accident occurred when a crowd watching a performance of the trick got out of control. The girl appeared on the Common dressed as a bride and several witnesses insisted that she had raised herself a considerable height above the ground.*"

— Barbara Comyns

Large eyes looking out from the coach.

A houseful of parrot, or a hand in a bushel of kittens.

Or else sent on an errand rushed in from the rain.

A kind place to dwell.

For protection she slept hovering some feet above the ground. This was remembered not as a dream, but as some peculiarity. The mechanism appears powdery; several times before there was nowhere to go. It was dark. There was a traveler with adequate room. A title approximate of a sink. The blew of youth had been trespassed, trampled by so many witnesses, and so skated.

I stood waiting at the edge of the frozen pond

followed by several earlier versions
Misgivings flew into three dark portraits on the wall.

This is the only way they could be seen.

A town defines talk. Sand is called water. This is the place having been taken out of the inhabitant, and then pasted all over the face in bright streaks which stick in green tissue paper.

She held violets to her fox complexion.

(One who was to sing or speak into a wind which would then carry the renouncement of mirror in other.)

Landscape reminder: those sparkles mistaken for fire opals are but reflections of a red day, which bends to distort the understanding of what is being said to whose waters. Gathers waves and mimics away. A receding shore can gather the eyeline.

The study of weather is conducted without instruments. A body is placed within elements. Evening, a period of decreasing daylight; a period of increasing night. Large eyes look down from the coach. They thought these instruments to deny a body refuge from the lessening of light and heat, that each heart cell could not sense the brooding form. A wash of dark color in a storm of horses. The eye thought to take the body home. The blew memory was constructed of watery images, none of which fit the carrier. And yet, the lessening of light would not permit her to stay at the edge of the frozen lake. The small glow of the carriage was enough to carry her away.

Alternatives to torchlight include other technologies in which suspension of vision is required. A switch is connected to a wire, and a bulb hidden within white walls. Her levitation was connected to a similar source with no physical outcasts or symptoms. Protection is a charm in which the swimmer may rise from the concoction of sleep, into a maze which brushes the ceiling.

There is a wood spell for such days to be repeated. Ocean swirl within third eye when there is no leaving. One speaks securely to trees, knowing they do not wander away or cast their eyes elsewhere. Branches remain a map. In every direction you can follow the air to which they point, and find the second spell which requires flight.

There was a dress in exchange for her keeping which looked different to her eyes in the glass than it did to those others staring. One image moved straight into the other melding, until blinking both became visible, as she tore it off of her body and ran out of the house and back into another night. No one had offered plural existence as one of few vehicles, but many had torn and run.

spell for housecleaning:

one: record mice, stairs, misfits
two: crowd

mice
stairs
fire
footsteps

and then repeat

Burnt in several circles the lavender circumspection.

The bracelet lay half woven on its thought. Uncurling was the pavement so summer rain not outburst but in diagonal waves, as if shipbound avenues. Mileage, the skeletal fragments broken animals in streetbacks. Inbound criteria: those who wish to be summoned will arrive or not arrive, and will be then cared for blinking in the light of the inner cavity where less is said and more is in retrospect, or less necessity for speech is not craving a table at which to drink or gesture.

There may be no physical location for meetings. They may be conducted silently and with fewer figures.

Safety is not careful carriage, and hears nothing but chants.

One present, two infused pasts, twenty-five futures using a technique of blustering. It is nine A. M. I arrange the immediate so as to be called a figure. Within windows and thoughts suppose mineral birth.

To explain a body, a unit of time dabbed dimly at pulse points. The shape of the earth is not monotone. These planed floors are not arches. A tent in order to think, in which a cove, a dive, or a suitcase. A place which supposed earth beneath. The memory of balance was not on planed floors. Nothing had been within the water themselves.

Sleep beside this alchemy. Lids flutter red or temperature. The bed floats which time begins. Bright within landslide, and memory blended boats, and when.

An hour is a furrow. A summer is one afternoon by a lake. Every evening wish: sky turns. Buildings wane pavement. Garments quiet, underwater. Sequin torso drifts and sleeps within a missing blue. Inner maze cannot be discerned from nodding stalks. A field of weight with wheat gone out. I walked into the ground without trying. Where silver finds water. Darkening lines taken within virtual. Someone vanishes, for space which is imagined, in the eye. Another may pull a wreath of clouds and guide them around her neck to find a river. You are somewhere, the unknown will say, and the summer will sign in waves.

Wind changes the size of eyes in watching a mist, and the motion of clouds obscuring a hill while driving. If both points are moving it becomes unclear whether it is the observer's motion or the actual clouds which are causing obscurity. And so to see becomes an island of sound and motion, this variable cloth through which threads may become blind interiors, or simple treads to be followed.

If a summer can be parted, watched, tended as air is not taught, then the sensation of fall air can also be carried until needed, and then unfolded on a patch of sunlight.

From the black spindly gathering of time among the mouths which are moving in weather, there are journals of time which cannot keep track. And yet they light rivers, and walk on roofs, and put down a shell as an ashtray, and walk ash-faced to the barefoot area, and sit among pillows and grapes, and are less comfortable than some and more comfortable than others.

They had just wandered from their parents' homes onto this island is shrinking. There are ashed faces of time among the mouths which are moving in weather who have not walls in which to return time. The street was the perfect job. The sympathetic head was shrinking, and the island was camping equipment.

Taste of green bitters befriended before winter, before the necessity of heat within the squat. One carries a child who will no longer walk. Something ended another began.

A maiden and laid waste. A tired motion began scattering seeds to one wind. One more which is whispering.

Closing eyes images come. There are the red and white edges which are memory. Explain, she will not, and had dropped the stir of waters by my side.

Within all of time is an undertime, a timewave which pulls. She does not challenge the ocean. No one remembers time, no one became a festival.

Is it the chamber where lashes sat sinking.

The past a mere flutter of palms. Light on a window. Sinking in rain messages which become bone and setting. Which becomes the edge of one flutter, the beginning of night. The cavity darkens until the memory of daylight is the dark space within water.

The past became a circle of songs.

My wrists were easy measuring, the smallness of bridges.

From what was once a moon and a time. A story of ice. Messages pour through time in incomplete rain. There is the heat which extends through fingers and walls, and this inhabited solitude in which no touch is infinitive.

Search urchins, web the foot trods of sullen believable magicians will not be banned drumming in the park. The laughable sunrise is not another day, it is the same day seamlessly, and that sensation of dying; to throw up arms and land in a pool is no longer a representation of what the senses perceive.

Rain, winds, strumming tide as silence. Side the shapes to come borrowing; an unknown knowledge was known (in the books whose lengths are not allowed to be willowing). The unsewn thought to which we wait on the banks murmuring *I have borrowed myself from earth*. I return these forms of ash. I wake within a storm of images whose lashes blink, awaken, and (just against my shoulder at noon or nine) rest beside my comfort. There is no boat within this lion. The postures have been sworn. You can walk into light without ornament. And the books whose lengths have been resung– they are allowed to bring home foxes without ever (as I neared wakefulness and remembered being on a boat with a lion) saying goodbye. The images that accompany them are many brooks old, and walk with the same riverbed eye, which remains somewhat open even in storm, and especially dreaming open into itself, which may appear closed to those who are looking, yet who would watch without wishing to (the one who is always killed in books because she has a pet fox, or because she would like to speak a long while to a brook). Say goodbye and (saying goodbye while some ornament was placed) also enter the riverbed eye and light a walk with tides. Heat July corresponds with foxes. This was written on a brow, and smudging somewhere else what had been undone could be movement just to leave somewhere else, but the dream persists which was imprinted upon sheets, and told to no cold morning. What Autumn had missed was not premonition but shelter. And now within a sweltering length which is allowed to be willing, although there is now no such thing as "allowed" or "not allowed," the willow would suggest an offering of sand, or intention dwelling there along a shore. (parentheses are crescents.)

ARCADE
Erica Hunt, poems
Alison Saar, drawings
1996, 56 pp., six images on vellum, $15,
    ISBN 0-932716-39-3
Limited signed edition with an original
    drawing, $125, ISBN 0-932716-40-7

THE WOMAN WITHOUT EXPERIENCES
Patricia Dienstfrey, prose-poem
1995, 134 pp., $12, ISBN 0-932716-37-7

STRIPPED TALES
Barbara Guest, poems
Anne Dunn, drawings
1995, 48 pp., 5 images on vellum, $14,
    ISBN 0-932716-36-9
Limited signed edition with an original
    drawing, $50, ISBN 0-932716-38-5

THE ROSY MEDALLIONS
Camille Roy, prose
1995, 69 pp., $10, ISBN 0-932716-35-0

DISTANCE WITHOUT DISTANCE
Barbara Einzig, prose
1994, 124 pp., $10, ISBN 0-932716-34-2

THE VIEW THEY ARRANGE
Dale Going, poems
1994, 72 pp., $10, ISBN 0-932716-33-4

JUST WHISTLE A VALENTINE
C. D. Wright, poems
Deborah Luster, photographs
1993, 64 pp., 6 photographs, $14,
    ISBN 0-932716-32-6

SPHERICITY
Mei-mei Berssenbrugge, poems
Richard Tuttle, drawings
1993, 48 pp., 7 drawings, $14,
    ISBN 0-932716-30-X
Limited signed edition with an original color
    drawing, $200, ISBN 0-932716-31-8

ISLE
Rena Rosenwasser, text
Kate Delos, drawings
1992, 56 pp., six color drawings, $12.95,
    ISBN 0-932716-28-8
Limited signed edition with an original color
    drawing, $40, ISBN 0-932716-29-6

UNDER FLAG
Myung Mi Kim, poems
1991, 56 pp., $9, ISBN 0-932716-27-X

PECULIAR MOTIONS
Rosmarie Waldrop, poems
Jennifer Macdonald, s/kins
1990, 48 pp., 4 images on vellum, $9,
    ISBN 0-932716-26-1
Limited signed edition with artist's
    original print, $35

BED OF LISTS
Elizabeth Robinson, poems
1990, 48 pp., $8, ISBN 0-932716-25-3

LIKE ROADS
Laura Moriarty, poems
1990, 74 pp., $8, ISBN 0-932716-24-5

MUSICALITY
Barbara Guest, poems
June Felter, drawings
1988, letterpress, 48 pp., 12 drawings,
    $9, ISBN 0-932716-23-7
Limited signed edition with hand-colored
    cover, $35

SMALL SALVATIONS
Patricia Dienstfrey, poems
1987, letterpress, 32 pp., $8,
    ISBN 0-932716-22-9
Limited signed edition with
    hand-colored cover, $35

SIMULACRA
Rena Rosenwasser, poems
Kate Delos, monoprints
1986, 49 pp., 14 color plates, $23,
    ISBN 0-932716-21-0
Limited signed edition, clothbound and
    sewn in signatures, $75

DESIRE$_1$
Thaisa Frank, prose
1982, 62 pp., $4.75, ISBN 0-932716-15-6

GRAMMARS FOR JESS
& TWENTY-TWO CROPPED SETS
Marina La Palma, poems
1981, 56 pp., $4.50, ISBN 0-932716-16-4

POEM FROM A SINGLE PALLET
Fanny Howe, poems
1980, 32 pp., $4.50, ISBN 0-932716-10-5

DREAMS IN HARRISON RAILROAD PARK
Nellie Wong, poems
1977, 48 pp., $6, ISBN 0-932716-14-8